Serving Others

BOOK SIX OF THE STUDIES IN CHRISTIAN LIVING

NAVPRESS ®

BRINGING TRUTH TO LIFE

OUR GUARANTEE TO YOU

The Navigators is an international Christian organization. Our mission is to reach, disciple, and equip people to know Christ and to make Him known through successive generations. We envision multitudes of diverse people in the United States and every other nation who have a passionate love for Christ, live a lifestyle of sharing Christ's love, and multiply spiritual laborers among those without Christ.

NavPress is the publishing ministry of The Navigators. NavPress publications help believers learn biblical truth and apply what they learn to their lives and ministries. Our mission is to stimulate spiritual formation among our readers.

© 1964 by The Navigators
Revised edition © 1981

ISBN 08910-90827

Printed in the United States of America

21 22 23 24 25 26 27 28 29 30 31 / 13 12 11 10 09 08 07 06 05 04

Yours to Give

Jesus told his disciples, "Freely you have received, freely give" (Matthew 10:8). We are expected to share the blessings we receive from the Lord.

Sharing with others should be one of the main results of your personal Bible study. As the Lord reveals to you new truths or personal applications, make a point to pass them on to others. The Holy Spirit will use you to challenge or encourage another Christian, or to awaken an unbeliever to his need of Christ.

To help you in further growth in discipleship, Book Six deals with these topics:

- Helping Others Find Christ
- Follow-up
- Power in Prayer
- Scriptural Giving
- World Vision

CHAPTER ONE

Helping Others Find Christ

1. Read Matthew 9:10. With what kind of people did Jesus associate?

   _____

2. Read John 3:16-18. Why did God send his Son into the world?

   _____

   What is <u>not</u> the reason Jesus came into the world, according to verse 17?

   _____

   What is necessary for us to escape condemnation? (verse 18)

   _____

3. Rewrite John 5:24 in your own words, as you would explain this verse to a non-Christian.

   _____

   _____

   _____

   _____

   _____

4. According to Jesus' teaching in John 6:44, why should we pray for God to draw our non-Christian friends to himself?

_____

_____

5. According to John 14:6, why is it important to present Jesus Christ to men and women who don't believe in him?

_____

_____

6. What did Peter say about Jesus in Acts 4:12?

_____

_____

7. In Acts 20:20, where did Paul say he met people to present Christ to them?

_____

8. Read Philippians 2:14-15. What can happen if we get rid of all our complaining and arguing?

_____

_____

_____

9. Read Colossians 4:5-6. What should be your behavior toward non-Christians?

_____

What should your speech be like?

_____

_____

Be ready to speak of Christ in any situation: Know the essentials of the gospel. Plan and practice how to explain about Christ in a clear and interesting way. Then pray and take advantage of your opportunities.

10. On the basis of the teaching in Hebrews 4:12, why do you think it is important to use the Scriptures when witnessing to non-Christians?

_____

_____

_____

11. Look up each reference listed in the left column, then read the statement next to it and check whether you think the statement is true or false.

		TRUE	FALSE
Proverbs 14:12	When it comes to spiritual matters, we can always trust our inner feelings.	☐	☐
Mark 8:36-37	Nothing in the world is more important than finding spiritual truth.	☐	☐
Romans 1:20	Anyone can learn at least something about God just by looking at the earth and the sky around us.	☐	☐
Romans 3:23	Only a few people in this world are sinless.	☐	☐
Romans 14:12	God can be safely ignored.	☐	☐

12. List here the names of the people you would most like to witness to. Pray for them, and plan how you can spend time with them. Then be alert for opportunities to talk with them about Jesus Christ.

_____

_____

_____

_____

_____

_____

CHAPTER TWO

Follow-Up

Follow-up means helping new believers get a good start in their Christian lives and in their growth toward spiritual maturity. Follow-up is the responsibility of all Christians. There is always someone who needs your help.

1. What can you learn from Matthew 10:29-31 about the value God places on every individual?

   _____

   _____

2. Read 1 Corinthians 4:14-15. Why did Paul feel personally responsible for the Corinthians?

   _____

   _____

3. What did Paul ask the Corinthians to do in 1 Corinthians 11:1?

   _____

   _____

4. What did Paul tell the Colossians he was praying for them in Colossians 1:9?

   _____

   _____

Paul's descriptions of his prayers for others in the New Testament serve as excellent scriptural models for our own intercession. Become familiar with these passages so you can use them frequently in praying for others: Ephesians 1:15-19 and 3:14-19; Philippians 1:3-6 and 1:9-11; and Colossians 1:9-12.

5. Read Colossians 1:28. In teaching others about Christ, what was Paul's goal?

_____

_____

6. Read 1 Thessalonians 2:7-8. How did Paul describe his way of teaching the Thessalonians to live the Christian life?

_____

_____

_____

_____

7. Read the following statements, and check all those which you think accurately reflect what you read in 1 Thessalonians 2:10-12.

☐ The lifestyle of Paul and his co-workers was a good example of true Christian living.
☐ Paul's attitude toward the Thessalonians was rooted in his understanding of God's ultimate aim for their lives.
☐ Paul knew the Thessalonians had been watching his way of life.
☐ Paul strove to help the Thessalonians focus their lives on God.

8. Read 1 Thessalonians 2:13. How did the Thessalonians respond to God's word?

_____

_____

_____

_____

9. What motivation for Paul's concern for the Thessalonian believers do you see expressed in 1 Thessalonians 3:5?

_____

_____

_____

10. Read 1 Timothy 4:12. In what areas did Paul say Timothy should set an example for the believers?

_____

_____

11. What did Paul tell Timothy to seek in 1 Timothy 6:11?

_____

_____

12. What do you learn from 2 Timothy 1:3 about Paul's concern for Timothy?

_____

_____

13. What did Timothy know about Paul, according to 2 Timothy 3:10-11?

_____

_____

_____

_____

14. Think of someone you would like to help grow in the Christian life. Remember to pray for him, and consider what more you can do to stimulate his growth. Should you spend more time with him? Consider meeting with him regularly in personal Bible study, using Book One of Studies in Christian Living. You may also want to take him with you as you witness to non-Christians or call on other young believers.

Summarize here how you would like to help this young Christian and what you intend to do.

_____

_____

_____

_____

_____

_____

_____

Power in Prayer

1. Read Psalm 107:1. Why should we give thanks to God?

_____

_____

2. What kind of prayer is taught in Psalm 113:1-3?

_____

3. What did Jesus teach about God in Matthew 7:9-11?

_____

_____

4. What did Jesus teach about prayer in Matthew 18:19?

_____

_____

5. How did Jesus show his submission to his Father in Matthew 26:39, which records his prayer on the night before he was crucified?

_____

_____

6. In Mark 1:35, at what time of day did Jesus pray?

_____

Where did he pray?

_____

7. What desire did Jesus have for his disciples, according
   to Luke 18:1?

   _____

   _____

8. Read the parable in Luke 18:9-14. What right attitude in
   prayer did Jesus teach in this story?

   _____

   _____

   _____

9. What did Jesus teach about prayer in John 16:24?

   _____

   _____

10. What did Jesus pray for his followers in John 17:24?

    _____

    _____

    _____

11. Read Acts 12:5. When Peter was put in prison, how did
    the Christians pray for him?

    _____

12. In Acts 16:25, what did Paul and Silas do after being
    beaten and imprisoned at Philippi?

    _____

13. What does Paul teach about prayer in Ephesians 6:18?

    _____

    _____

    _____

    _____

14. What kind of prayer is taught in Hebrews 13:15?

_____

15. What wrong attitude in prayer does James write against in James 4:3?

_____

_____

16. What qualities for effective prayer are taught in 1 Peter 4:7?

_____

17. Choose one or more of these passages, and rewrite it in your own words as a personal prayer to God.

Psalm 30:1-3
Psalm 51:10-12
Psalm 61:3-5
Psalm 139:23-24
Psalm 145:1-3

_____

_____

_____

_____

_____

_____

_____

_____

_____

_____

_____

_____

_____

CHAPTER FOUR

Scriptural Giving

As those who are accountable to God, we should use in a responsible way all that God has given us.

1. Read Deuteronomy 8:17-18. What is a natural way to feel about our money and possessions? (verse 17)

   _____

   _____

   Where does the ability to produce wealth actually come from? (verse 18)

   _____

2. What can we do with our wealth, according to Proverbs 3:9?

   _____

3. Read Matthew 6:2-4. According to what Jesus taught, who should know about what we have given?

   _____

4. Read Matthew 6:19-21. What kind of wealth should we seek?

   _____

   _____

Why is this important? (verse 21)

_____

_____

5. According to Jesus' words in Matthew 6:31-33, why
   should we not worry about food and clothing?

_____

_____

What instead should be our first concern?

_____

6. Read Jesus' final statement in Matthew 19:21 to the rich
   young man, and observe the man's response in verse
   22. Was Jesus trying to make this man poor or rich?

_____

What did Jesus say in verses 23-24?

_____

_____

_____

Why do you think this is true?

_____

_____

_____

7. Read Mark 12:41-44. What did Jesus mean when he
   said the poor widow gave more than the others?

_____

_____

_____

_____

_____

8. How would you summarize the truth of Luke 6:38?

_____

_____

_____

9. What did Jesus warn about in Luke 12:15?

_____

_____

10. Read the parable Jesus told in Luke 12:16-21. Why was this man foolish?

_____

_____

What do you think it means to be "rich toward God" (verse 21)?

_____

_____

_____

11. What words of Jesus are recorded in Acts 20:35?

_____

_____

12. According to 2 Corinthians 8:9, what example did Jesus set for us?

_____

_____

_____

13. What correct attitude in giving is taught in 2 Corinthians 9:7?

_____

What wrong attitudes are mentioned?

_____

14. What did Paul teach about giving in Galatians 6:6?

_____

_____

15. Read 1 Timothy 6:9. What happens to people who desire to be rich?

_____

_____

_____

16. Rewrite 1 Timothy 6:10 in your own words.

_____

_____

_____

_____

_____

17. Read Hebrews 10:34. Why did these people accept joyfully the confiscation of their property?

_____

_____

18. Read Hebrews 13:5. Instead of loving money, what should our attitude be, and why?

_____

_____

_____

19. According to 1 Peter 4:10, how should we use the gifts we have received?

_____

_____

_____

20. Summarize here the most important things you studied in this chapter.

_____

_____

_____

_____

_____

_____

Many Christians have found a regular plan for giving to be both scriptural and practical. Planning ensures against irregular or unwise giving, and also against neglect. In a day when so many demands are made on your time and money, planned giving helps you honor the Lord with your possessions.

Your plan should include these steps:
1. Thoughtfully decide what percentage of your income you will return to the Lord—a minimum percentage.
2. Set aside the Lord's portion first whenever you receive money. Put this aside to be used as he leads; once set aside it is his and should not be used for other purposes.
3. Prayerfully distribute the Lord's money as he directs. It is usually good to do this at a regular time—weekly or monthly.

Make extra gifts and increase your giving as God increases your faith, and as he prospers you. As you trust God with your material resources, he will entrust you with his spiritual resources.

The person who dedicates his money to God is dedicating himself—the fruit of his time, talent, and energy. One who fails to dedicate his money has not fully committed himself to God.

World Vision

The Lord's concern is for the entire world, and this should be our concern as well.

1. What did the Lord promise Abraham in Genesis 22:18?

   _____

   _____

   _____

2. In the statement of God's control over the world in Psalm 22:27-28, what response to him by the nations is foretold?

   _____

   _____

   _____

3. What truth is taught in Psalm 24:1?

   _____

   _____

4. What prophecy about the world is made in Habakkuk 2:14?

   _____

5. What did Jesus command his disciples in Matthew 28:19-20?

_____

_____

_____

_____

6. How did John the Baptist describe Jesus in John 1:29?

_____

_____

7. What is God's attitude toward the world, according to John 3:16?

_____

8. What did Jesus say about himself in John 8:12?

_____

_____

9. According to John 14:31, what message was Jesus demonstrating to the world?

_____

_____

10. Read 2 Corinthians 5:18-20. How does God communicate his message to the world?

_____

_____

What is his message?

_____

_____

_____

Remember to pray. Many of us cannot reach other nations on our feet, but we can reach them on our knees.

11. According to the prophecy in Revelation 7:9, where do God's worshipers in heaven come from?

_____

_____

12. What is prophesied about all nations in Revelation 15:4?

_____

_____

13. After reviewing your answers in this chapter, what conclusions can you make regarding:

God's plan for the world?

_____

_____

_____

_____

_____

Your responsibility to the world?

_____

_____

_____

_____

_____

"God was reconciling the world to himself in Christ" (2 Corinthians 5:19).

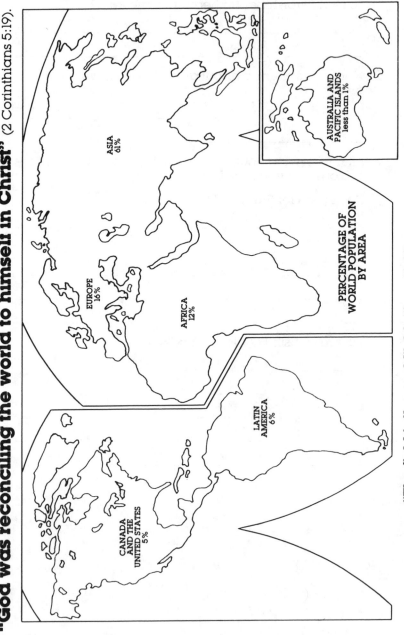

ASIA
61%

EUROPE
16%

AFRICA
12%

CANADA
AND THE
UNITED STATES
5%

LATIN
AMERICA
6%

AUSTRALIA AND
PACIFIC ISLANDS
less than 1%

PERCENTAGE OF
WORLD POPULATION
BY AREA

"The field is the world" (Matthew 13:38).